Feedback:

Giving It, Receiving It

FOUNDED 1870

About the Authors

Shirley Poertner is the president of Poertner Consulting Group, a consulting and training firm specializing in organizational development and individual learning. She has more than 15 years of experience in the training and development field. Ms. Poertner has worked with numerous public-sector agencies as well as Fortune 500 companies.

Karen Massetti Miller is the Editor in Chief of American Media's How-To Book Series. Her experience as both a teacher and practitioner of business and professional communication has given her insight into the nature and importance of effective feedback.

Adapted for the American Correctional Association by **Ida M. Halasz**, Ph.D., who served as the Deputy Administrator of the National Institute of Corrections Academy, U.S. Department of Justice. Currently, as Vice President of Powell International Inc., she provides training and consulting services to public and private sector organizations.

ISBN 1-56991-087-1

Foreword

I have long maintained that corrections is a "people business." I make a point of addressing all new staff and supervisors working in our multi-security level prison of 1,250 prisoners soon after they begin their assignments. In my address one theme is constant: corrections is a people business and in order to have a successful career in corrections you really have to like working with people. A good "people person" has good communication skills. Employees need to value communications as a critical tool and become proficient with this skill, just as they must learn to become proficient in using other critical tools such as computers, radios, weapons and keys.

Feedback is an important facet to communicating. It provides answers to the most commonly asked question, "How am I doing?" For staff, their supervisors and prisoners, feedback is essential for learning new behaviors and skills, maintaining morale, and creating an atmosphere for an effective organization. Feedback not only communicates what can be improved upon, but also what is being done right. Feedback is important for the growth of the organization at all levels, starting with prisoners and moving right up the chain of command to the Warden.

The American Correctional Association is dedicated to the advancement of professionals working in the field. To that end, ACA supports, develops and provides training to assist employees in improving their job skills. In a time when burgeoning prison populations have created more intense scrutiny of dollars and resources than at any other time in history, facilities are looking for the most cost-effective use of training dollars possible. New skills cannot be effectively internalized in a single training session, however. They must be honed through repetition and practice. This workbook can serve as an outline for a classroom training session or as a self-directed study course. Upon completion, it will also serve as reference for employees' use after the training session ends and when the real learning begins.

Luella R. Burke, Warden
Saginaw Correctional Facility—Michigan Department of Corrections
Chair—Women Working in Corrections Committee, ACA

a publication of the
AMERICAN CORRECTIONAL ASSOCIATION
4380 Forbes Boulevard
Lanham, Maryland 20706-4322
(301) 918-1800
Fax: (301) 918-1900
http://www.corrections.com/ACA

Introduction

Good communication tops most people's list of important workplace skills. Though correctional organizations are increasing the use of complex electronic equipment, not all of the information staff need is found on-line and in databases. Effective person-to-person communication is important as correctional organizations grow or downsize and change to meet new challenges.

One of the most important person-to-person communication skills is the ability to give and receive feedback effectively. It is also one of the most challenging. No amount of sophisticated technology can diminish the anxiety supervisors and staff feel when faced with a feedback session. Perhaps you have experienced this sense of apprehension, and that's why you're reading this workbook.

The good news is that feedback doesn't have to be painful. By learning the proven techniques presented here, you can develop your feedback skills. If you provide feedback to others—staff, co-workers, or your manager—this workbook will help you to present your ideas more effectively. It will also help you to be a better receiver of feedback, even feedback that is presented awkwardly. With just a little practice, you'll be able to turn feedback sessions into tools that can help you (and your co-workers) improve your (their) job performance and meet important goals. Good luck!

Assessing Your Current Feedback Skills
How to Get the Most from This Workbook

This workbook is designed to help you improve your skills in giving and receiving feedback in the correctional workplace. As you read, think about the ways in which you give and receive feedback. Ask yourself whether you recognize your own behaviors in the examples and whether there are feedback skills you can develop further. To help you identify skills you would like to improve, here are two self-assessments to evaluate your current feedback skills—one for how you give feedback and another for how you receive it.

How Well Do I Give Feedback?

This self-assessment will help you measure your current skills in *giving feedback*. For each statement, check "Rarely," "Sometimes," or "Often" to indicate how consistently you use the described behavior in the workplace.

		Rarely	Sometimes	Often
1.	I pick an appropriate time and place to give feedback.	____	____	____
2.	I keep my emotions in check, remaining calm and keeping my voice even.	____	____	____
3.	I provide specific, detailed information about the staff member's behavior or performance.	____	____	____
4.	I explain the affect the staff member's actions are having on others or the organization.	____	____	____
5.	I really listen to the responses of those receiving my feedback.	____	____	____
6.	I clarify my expectations if there is any confusion about the behavior in question.	____	____	____
7.	I remember to thank and encourage the receivers of my feedback.	____	____	____

		Rarely	Sometimes	Often
8.	I provide input as needed in developing an action plan for meeting behavioral or performance goals.	____	____	____
9.	I focus on the steps of the feedback process to keep the dialogue on track.	____	____	____
10.	I try to understand feedback from the other person's point of view and preferred communication style.	____	____	____

Of course, *giving feedback is only half of the story*. Take a moment now and assess your skills as a feedback recipient.

How Well Do I Receive Feedback?

This self-assessment will help you measure your current skills in *receiving feedback*. For each statement, check "Rarely," "Sometimes," or "Often" to indicate how consistently you use the described behavior in the workplace.

		Rarely	Sometimes	Often
1.	I truly listen to what "feedback givers" are saying.	____	____	____
2.	I keep feedback in perspective and don't overreact.	____	____	____
3.	I try to learn from all feedback, even if it's poorly given.	____	____	____
4.	I am willing to admit to and learn from questions about my performance or behavior at work.	____	____	____
5.	Rather than avoiding feedback, I attempt to turn every feedback session into a useful encounter.	____	____	____
6.	I accept redirection and reinforcement rather than denying them.	____	____	____
7.	I accept responsibility for my role in achieving individual, team, and organizational goals.	____	____	____

	Rarely	Sometimes	Often
8. I accept responsibility for searching for solutions to performance and behavioral problems that threaten goals.	_____	_____	_____
9. I accept responsibility for keeping my emotions in check during feedback discussions.	_____	_____	_____
10. I am committed to listening and learning in all feedback situations.	_____	_____	_____

How Did You Score?

How did you score on the two self-assessments? If you answered most of the questions with "Often," your skills for giving feedback and receiving feedback effectively are well developed.

If you answered a number of questions with "Rarely" or "Sometimes," your feedback skills could probably use further development.

At the end of this workbook, we will give you an opportunity to reassess your skills. You also will have an opportunity to develop an action plan for strengthening those areas in which you need more experience.

Table of Contents

Chapter Five

Steps for Receiving Feedback Effectively

Chapter Six

Feedback and Communication Styles

Chapter Seven

Handling Difficult Feedback Situations

Chapter Eight

Developing Your Feedback Skills

Chapter One

THE POWER OF FEEDBACK

Chapter Objectives

After completing this chapter, you should be able to:

- Define feedback.

- Identify three ineffective types of feedback.

- Identify the traits of effective feedback.

- Define redirection and reinforcement, two types of feedback that are especially effective in the workplace.

What Is Feedback?

A division manager hands in a report to her regional director and waits for a month without receiving a reaction. The division manager wonders, "What did I do wrong?"

A supervisor becomes upset at a clerical staff member who consistently makes spelling errors. "Don't you know anything about the English language?" he yells. "It's amazing you ever finished high school!" The supervisor slams a recently typed memo on the clerk's desk and stalks off; the specific errors are never discussed.

A staff member receives praise from a supervisor during an annual evaluation. "You're doing a great job," she's told. "Keep up the good work." As the staff member leaves the supervisor's office, she wonders, "What exactly am I doing well? I want to keep doing it, but I'm not sure what 'it' is."

Feedback . . .
- **Positive**
- **Negative**

Whenever we respond to another person, we are giving that person **feedback**. We may be responding to any number of things:

- The way a person looks
- His or her actions
- Something he or she said
- A combination of factors

Similarly, our feedback may take many forms. We may state our responses verbally, through speaking or writing. Or, we may react nonverbally, letting our body language—such as facial expressions—speak for us.

Though there are many types of feedback, not all feedback is useful. Consider our three examples. In the first example, the regional director has responded to the division manager with *silence*. Silence is actually one of the most common forms of feedback in the workplace. How many times have you heard a supervisor say, "You won't hear from me unless there's a problem"? But silence can be misinterpreted. In this case, the division manager has interpreted silence as criticism, but is that what the regional director really means? The regional director may just have thought she was too busy to respond, yet her silence has sent a message that is unintentionally negative.

Silence certainly wasn't a problem for the supervisor in the second example. That supervisor chose to give feedback in the form of *criticism*, attacking the clerk's personal qualities rather than focusing on the typing errors. The supervisor may have vented some emotion by yelling at the clerk. But the clerk still has no idea what the errors are and what should be done about them. The supervisor's criticism has only created distrust and hostility, which will make it even more difficult to discuss the actual problem.

> Whenever we respond to another person, we are giving that person feedback.

The supervisor in the third example offered *praise*, certainly a more pleasant form of feedback than the first two. The staff member in the third example is undoubtedly happy to learn that her boss likes her work. But unless she asks for more specific details about what actions she should continue, the praise is of little long-term value.

As you can see, we are constantly responding to the actions of others, sometimes even without meaning to—as the old cliché says, "You cannot not communicate." How can we ensure that our responses provide people with useful feedback? Our first step is to determine what we want our feedback to accomplish.

Take a Moment . . .

Did the opening examples remind you of a similar situation you may have encountered?

Describe a situation where you *received* poor or vague feedback.

_____

_____

_____

Do you think the situation you experienced was handled well? How might it have been handled better? _____

_____

_____

Now describe a situation in which you *gave* poor or vague feedback to a staff member or offender. _____

_____

_____

_____

How do you think you could have handled the situation better?

_____

_____

How Do We Give Feedback in the Workplace?

Workplace feedback—information we provide fellow staff about their job performance and their work-related behavior to help them meet individual, group, and organizational goals.

In the workplace, our feedback takes on special meaning. In this workbook, we will define **workplace feedback** as: information we provide fellow staff about their acts to help them meet individual, group, and organizational goals. In the workplace, there are two types of acts for which we generally provide feedback: job performance and work-related behavior.

- **Job performance** involves competency—whether or not an employee is capably performing specific tasks that have been assigned.

- **Work-related behavior** involves the way in which a staff member performs his or her tasks—whether he or she speaks politely to offenders, for example—and works cooperatively with other team members.

Notice that our definition of workplace feedback is fairly specific. When we give workplace feedback, we are not commenting on our co-workers' personalities or private lives. We also are not dwelling on staff's past errors. Instead, we are responding to those factors that affect our feedback recipient's work or the work of others so that our recipient can plan for the future.

What is the best way to give workplace feedback? As we have seen, not all types of information result in effective feedback. The feedback given in our first three examples produced a variety of results. Silence allowed the division manager to create her own interpretation of the regional director's response, which may or may not have been correct. Criticism created harsh feelings between the clerk and the supervisor. Praise created positive feelings during the staff member's evaluation but accomplished nothing more. What could more effective feedback have done?

Redirection and Reinforcement

Think for a moment about our last two examples. Did the supervisor really want to insult the clerk? No, the criticism was meant to **redirect** the clerk's job performance—it just came out badly. And what was the intention of the supervisor in the second example? To **reinforce** the staff member's positive actions so that she would repeat and develop them.

These two types of feedback—redirection and reinforcement—are especially effective in the workplace.

- **Redirection**—identifies job-related behaviors and performance that do not contribute to individual, group, and organizational goals; helps the staff member develop alternative strategies.

- **Reinforcement**—identifies job-related behaviors and performance that contribute to individual, group, and organizational goals; encourages the staff member to repeat and develop them.

Redirection and reinforcement are really two halves of the same coin—they work together to provide staff with the information they need to improve their job performance and work up to their full potential. When feedback takes the form of redirection and reinforcement, it has a number of useful traits:

- It is focused on acts, not attitude.
- It is directed toward the future.
- It is goal- oriented.
- It is multidirectional.
- It is supportive.
- It is continual.

Useful Feedback Is Focused on Acts, Not Attitude

Useful workplace feedback focuses on acts rather than a staff member's attitude or personal traits—it responds to specific actions that are done in the process of performing one's job. Attacking someone's talent and abilities, educational background, physical attributes, or ethnic background is not useful feedback. In extreme cases, it could leave your organization subject to legal action.

Sometimes, we may think that we are giving a person feedback about his or her actions when, in fact, we are commenting on attitude—which is not a useful type of feedback. It does little good to accuse an employee of being "unenthusiastic" or "unprofessional." We have no way of knowing how that person truly feels, nor is it really our business. Instead, we should focus on what we can see—the acts that we hope to redirect or reinforce. For example, we don't comment on someone's lack of professionalism. We *redirect* job performance issues, like spelling errors, and behavioral problems that affect job performance, like lateness.

Take a Moment . . .

Think of a situation in which you received redirection that was not focused on acts (like the clerical example at the beginning of this chapter). Describe the criticism you received. How did the other person approach you? What did he or she say?

_____

_____

_____

_____

_____

_____

_____

How did you respond to this criticism? Were there aspects of your work that could have been improved? How could your "feedback giver" have changed his or her message—so that you could have benefited from the advice by redirecting your efforts?

_____

_____

_____

_____

_____

_____

_____

Useful Feedback Is Directed Toward the Future

The purpose of feedback is not to dwell on the past—it is to plan for the future. Though feedback begins with a consideration of past and current behaviors and job performance, it certainly doesn't end there. Useful feedback uses past actions as a springboard to help the feedback recipient develop effective plans for future actions.

Useful Feedback Is Goal Oriented

Everyone within your organization shares common goals that relate to your organization's mission, vision, and strategies for success. Members of your team or department share certain goals as well. Similarly, everyone in your organization has individual goals that will help him or her contribute to the organization's goals.

We might think of individual goals as paths all leading to the completion of organizational goals. As each of us walks along our path, we believe that we are moving in the right direction. But there may be obstacles ahead that we can't see, or perhaps our path is interfering with someone else's. The only way we will ever know these things is if people from other vantage points tell us. When we look at feedback this way, it becomes as important a work tool as a security device or computer.

Take a Moment . . .

Think of an instance when a co-worker or a supervisor provided feedback from his or her vantage point. Describe the instance.

_____

_____

_____

Did the feedback get you back on track toward meeting an important goal? If so, what was the goal? _____

How did the feedback help you in other ways?

_____

_____

Useful Feedback Is Multidirectional

Many of us might think of feedback as hierarchical in nature: a manager or supervisor sends feedback downward to a staff member, not the other way around. But feedback is multidirectional. In a hierarchical organization, staff need to send feedback upward to managers. Otherwise, administration will have no way of knowing what is actually happening on the front lines. Staff also need to provide feedback laterally to co-workers so that problems can be corrected immediately instead of waiting for administration to respond.

As teams have become more common in correctional organizations, ongoing feedback among all team members is especially important. Because every member of the team has a different perspective, each person has a unique vantage point and insight into the work situation. Sharing information from one perspective can help other team members see things they might not have seen from their vantage points. It is everyone's responsibility to share his or her unique insights in order to help the team meet its goal.

Take a Moment . . .

Whose behavior or performance affects how you are able to do your job? Certainly your supervisor. Who else? List them below by position or role. (Don't forget to include those external to your workplace, as well as internal contacts, such as offenders or inmates.)

_____   _____

_____   _____

_____   _____

1. Identify with a "*" the role you would be most likely to provide with reinforcing feedback.

2. Identify with a "#" the role you would most likely to provide with redirecting feedback.

Useful Feedback Is Supportive

Useful feedback is given in a spirit of supportiveness. The sole purpose of giving workplace feedback is to help staff, supervisors, and co-workers improve the quality of their work in order to meet goals. It is always given with helpfulness in mind. Feedback should never be given in a way that belittles the recipient or makes others look good at that person's expense.

Useful Feedback Is Continual

Feedback isn't just something we provide during an annual review or some other type of formal evaluation. In order to do our jobs in the best way possible, we need continual information about our job-related behaviors and performance. We need to know immediately when we should redirect our efforts so that simple mistakes don't become costly errors. We also need reinforcement when those changes have been successful so that we can continue to develop a specific action.

When feedback is continual, staff members feel comfortable responding to each other on an ongoing basis. As we develop solutions to specific situations, redirecting feedback leads to reinforcing feedback. Each new piece of information brings us closer to meeting our individual and group goals, as the diagram below shows.

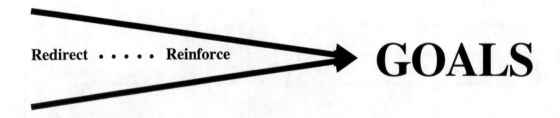

Redirect · · · · · Reinforce → **GOALS**

Misperceptions About Feedback

As useful as feedback can be, many of us are reluctant to give it or receive it. Usually that reluctance is based on misperceptions we have about feedback. Though we are learning to see feedback in a more positive light, we still associate feedback with hurtful criticism. We are reluctant to hurt the feelings of others, and they certainly don't want their own work to be criticized. Perhaps you can recall times in your life when you have been the subject of hurtful criticism—or times when your criticism, no matter how well intentioned, seemed to hurt the feelings of another.

When we think about the times we have received hurtful criticism, we often find that what hurt us wasn't that someone commented on our work. What hurt us was the *way* in which those comments were offered. Somehow, feedback about our errors in our reports or in our cell searches turned into an evaluation of our entire educational history and personality.

As we've seen, effective feedback doesn't veer off into these types of unstructured statements. By following the steps in this workbook, you will be able to provide feedback that avoids hurtful criticism. You also will be able to respond to any hurtful criticism you may receive so that it, too, becomes useful.

Share the Benefits of Continual Feedback

When staff learn to provide and expect feedback that is focused on acts, directed toward the future, goal-oriented, multidirectional, supportive, and continual, you will find that feedback sessions become opportunities for creative problem solving—rather than dreaded encounters. You, your co-workers, and supervisors will share the same language, and you will be able to share ideas without fear of hurt feelings or reprisals.

You are beginning to realize that continual feedback can have a number of benefits for you and your organization. But you still may not be totally comfortable with the idea. In the next chapter, we will explore some of the common misperceptions that keep people from giving feedback.

Chapter One Review

Suggested answers appear on page 94.

1. Workplace feedback is information we provide co-workers and supervisors about their _____ and _____ behavior.

2. Three types of *ineffective* workplace feedback are:

    _____

    _____

    _____

3. Two types of *effective* workplace feedback are:

    _____

    _____

4. Effective workplace feedback has a number of traits. Three of them are:

    _____

    _____

    _____

Chapter Two

USEFUL FEEDBACK IS DETAILED FEEDBACK

Chapter Objectives

After completing this chapter, you should be able to:

- Describe the importance of detailed feedback.

- Identify the features of detailed feedback.

- Identify the roles that those giving and receiving feedback play in creating detailed feedback.

Create Detailed Feedback

In Chapter One, we defined workplace feedback as: information we provide fellow co-workers and staff we supervise about their job performance and their work-related behavior to help them meet individual, group, and organizational goals. We've already seen that the *nature* of the information helps determine whether our feedback will be effective or not. Effective feedback focuses on *acts* rather than attitudes, is *goal-oriented*, and is always given in a *spirit of mutual support*.

> **Feedback:**
> - **Focuses on acts**
> - **Is goal-oriented**
> - **Is given in a spirit of mutual support**

Another key feature that helps make feedback effective is the amount of detail it provides. Feedback is most helpful when it provides as much detailed information about our actions as possible. We can make sure that feedback is detailed by remembering these simple guidelines:

- Detailed feedback is specific.

- Detailed feedback is accurate.

- Detailed feedback is inquiring.

Detailed Feedback Is Specific

"I just don't like the way you handled that inmate!"

"The report you wrote just doesn't make sense. You know what I mean."

"Try to put a little more 'oomph' in your staff training sessions. Wake people up!"

You've probably heard statements like these before. They are attempts at redirection, but they're poor ones. They don't give the person receiving the feedback enough specific information to make changes in his or her actions. The most the receiver can do in each case is to try again. But without specific information, the attempt will be just another shot in the dark. The receiver may have to make several attempts before he or she hits on something the person giving the feedback likes. This is a waste of time and resources as well as a drain on morale.

You can avoid situations like this by making your feedback as specific as possible. Before giving feedback to another person, recall as much specific information as you can about the action you want to redirect or reinforce. You might begin by asking yourself what, when, where, who, and how:

- What happened?

- Where and when did it occur?

- Who was involved?

- How did it affect others?

With these questions in mind, consider this

Guidelines for detailed feedback:
- specific
- accurate
- inquiring

---

alternative to our third example:

"Your training sessions always include a wealth of good information, but you don't sound personally excited about the things you're presenting. Your voice is often very soft and monotone, and your rate of speaking is very slow. The evaluations show that the participants think you sound bored with your topic, and that makes them feel bored, too. Are there some things you could do to make your enthusiasm for your topic more evident to the participants?"

This revised example tells the feedback recipient *specifically what* he's been doing (not projecting enthusiasm for his material), *where* and *when* he's been doing it (during presentations), *who* it involves (his listeners), and *how* it affects the participants (makes them feel bored). The recipient will be able to redirect his efforts with much less confusion and effort than if he had received the feedback in our earlier example.

It is also important to be specific when giving reinforcing feedback. Consider the difference between these two statements:

"Great report, Karl. Keep up the good work."

"I liked the way you incorporated the two graphs into your report this month, Karl. They made it much easier to follow the inmate population. I hope you'll do it again."

Karl will be better able to repeat his report-writing efforts based on the specific information in the second example.

Detailed Feedback Is Accurate

Feedback can do little good if it inaccurately portrays the action in question. Describing actions that were never taken—or events that never occurred—only puts your feedback recipient on the defensive as he or she attempts to describe what really took place.

Always be sure that you have an accurate knowledge of the situation you are describing before you begin a feedback session. If you think that there might be some question about your version of the situation, identify more than one instance of it and document times, dates, and locations. You can also check your observations against those of others to see if you all arrive at similar interpretations.

Detailed Feedback Is Inquiring

Have an inquiring mind. Learn all that you can about a complicated situation before you give feedback. Your investigation may help you arrive at a totally different interpretation of the situation—an interpretation that could result in totally different feedback. You may determine that you wish to direct your feedback to a different person. You might even determine that actions you thought needed to be changed were actually making a positive contribution.

Continue to ask questions during the feedback process itself. Encourage your feedback recipient to describe events that may be affecting the situation in question, and involve him or her in developing any plans for future action.

Take a Moment . . .

Effective feedback is *specific*. The person giving the following feedback could have been more specific in reinforcing or redirecting the other person's performance or behavior. Write a response that is more effective.

"Pat, this report is not clear."

_____

_____

"Doug, your unit seems to be working well together."

_____

_____

Effective feedback is *accurate*. Describe a situation in which you need to give feedback to someone. Identify three situations in which the behavior has occurred. Be sure to give the times, dates, and locations. _____

_____

_____

_____

Effective feedback is *inquiring*. Describe an instance when your inquiries—either prior to or during a feedback discussion—resulted in information that greatly changed the focus of the feedback you planned to deliver. _____

_____

_____

Don't Let Time Dull Your Details

Time has a way of dulling even the most vivid memories. To incorporate as many details into your feedback as possible, give redirection or reinforcement as close as possible to the time the act in question actually occurred. It is always easier to discuss something when events are fresh in everyone's mind. In addition, responding to a situation quickly shows that you believe that it is important.

One exception to this rule is the situation in which you need to both reinforce and redirect the person receiving the feedback. People receiving both types of feedback generally focus on the redirection. The reinforcement that you wanted to provide often is ignored.

To alleviate this confusion, try splitting your feedback. One effective method of splitting feedback is to give reinforcement as soon after the action in question as possible. Then provide redirection closer to the time the person is going to repeat the action. For example, a manager has just received a monthly report. She can reinforce her staff member's use of charts and bar graphs immediately after receiving the report. Then she can redirect the staff member closer to next month's report due date. She can ask the staff member to also include a spread sheet with the report.

A word of caution—balance the need for a timely response against the need to prepare for the feedback session. Remember that your feedback needs to be well organized, documented and on time. Beginning to plan your feedback as soon as you realize that a situation requires your response will help you to be both well prepared and on time.

Feedback—A Two-Way Process

Giving Feedback: The Process of Specifying

Keeping these guidelines in mind as you prepare your feedback will help you develop redirection and reinforcement that is detailed and useful. As you begin your first feedback sessions, you might think of giving detailed feedback as the process of *specifying*—that is, providing more and more specific information to the person receiving your feedback. The more specific the information you can provide, the closer your recipient can come to meeting individual, group, and organizational goals.

Creating useful feedback isn't only the responsibility of the person giving feedback. Both those giving feedback and those receiving it have important roles to play in ensuring that feedback provides as much useful detail as possible.

Receiving Feedback: The Process of Probing

It's a fact of life—you won't always receive useful, detailed feedback on the job. But that doesn't mean you have to accept poor quality feedback that does nothing to help you redirect or reinforce your own performance. Feedback recipients can request the details they need through the process of *probing*—asking the person giving the feedback for more details. As you probe for information, you will receive more and more specific details about your behavior and performance.

The following diagram illustrates how the processes of specifying and probing work together to bring ever-increasing amounts of information to the feedback situation. As the levels of probing and specifying increase, so does the level of detailed information available to the person receiving the feedback—which will help the person move closer to achieving goals.

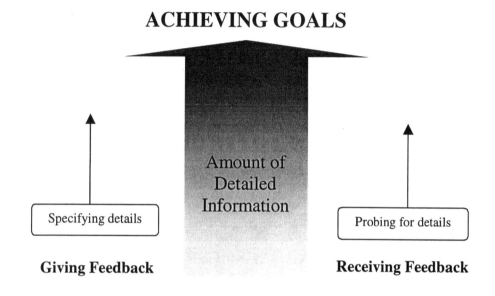

ACHIEVING GOALS

Amount of Detailed Information

Specifying details

Probing for details

Giving Feedback   **Receiving Feedback**

**More details from specifying or probing =
More information =
More help to achieve your personal and
work goals**

In the following chapters, we will outline specific techniques that will help you to be an efficient giver and receiver of feedback. In each case, we will stress the importance of specifying and probing for the amount of information necessary to redirect or reinforce behaviors and performance.

Chapter Two Review

Suggested answers appear on page 94 and 95.

1. What are three traits of detailed feedback?

   _____

   _____

   _____

2. In order to provide your feedback recipient with as much specific detail as possible, when should you provide reinforcement or redirection?

   _____

   _____

   _____

3. What is specifying?

   _____

   _____

   _____

4. What is probing?

   _____

   _____

   _____

Chapter Three

PLANNING EFFECTIVE FEEDBACK

Chapter Objectives

After completing this chapter, you should be able to:

- Describe the importance of planning feedback.

- Prepare detailed feedback by asking yourself a series of questions.

Why You Should Plan Your Feedback

Effective feedback doesn't just happen. Whether you're giving redirection or reinforcement, you should plan what you are going to say in advance. You will need to identify examples to support the redirection or reinforcement you want to give. You also need to organize your thoughts so that you are able to present your feedback coherently.

As you take part in more and more feedback sessions, sometimes you may actually spend more time planning your feedback than you do giving it. This is not uncommon—the more time you put into your planning, the more smoothly your feedback sessions will run.

> . . . the more time you put into your planning, the more smoothly your feedback sessions will run.

Ask These Questions When Planning Feedback

Knowing that you want to give someone reinforcement or redirection is just the beginning of the feedback planning process. Try asking yourself this series of questions to get your feedback planning on track.

- Can I identify and accurately describe the behavior or performance I want to redirect or reinforce and its influence on others in the organization?

- Do I have detailed examples of the act and its influence that I can use to support my descriptions?

- Can I identify and describe the results that I hope my reinforcement or redirection will produce?

- Does the person receiving the feedback understand my expectations for his or her performance?

- Is the person receiving the feedback really responsible for the act in question?

- Is the other person open to receiving feedback from me?

- Have I put off giving this feedback for a long time?

- Have I given myself enough time to prepare the feedback?

Identifying Behavior and Performance Issues

Can you identify and accurately describe the specific behavior or performance you want to redirect or reinforce and its influence on others in the organization? As we saw in Chapter Two, effective feedback requires more than just a vague statement that you like or dislike someone's work. Statements like "Something's wrong here—I don't know exactly what it is, but change it" don't provide enough details for staff members to begin to redirect their actions. Likewise, telling someone, "Keep up the good work!" does little to tell that person what good work is.

Begin your feedback preparation by identifying the specific job performance or behavior issue you want to redirect or reinforce. Also identify the influence the act has on others in your organization. Prepare for your feedback sessions by making a list in which you describe the act and its influence, as in these two examples:

Redirection

Behavior to Redirect:

Kelsey was late to work three times in the past week.

Influence on Others:

Person on previous shift had to work late; people on same shift are irritated and demoralized.

Reinforcement

Performance to Reinforce:

Reorganized work process so that correspondence is completed more quickly and with fewer errors.

Influence on Others:

Lower turnaround time means we can respond more quickly; reduction in errors means fewer documents have to be redone, which also saves time and money.

Providing Examples

Do you have detailed examples of the act and its influence that you can use to support your argument? The more examples you can describe, the stronger your case will be—especially if you are asking someone to redirect an action and are concerned that the person might resist your redirection. Here is one way you could list examples of actions and influences to support redirection of the employee who is late to work:

Example of Behavior	Influence on Others
Monday: Kelsey 1/2 hour late for first shift.	*Roland had to operate by himself.*
Wednesday: Kelsey 20 minutes late getting back from lunch.	*Roland had to delay lunch break; unit short-staffed at busiest time of day.*
Thursday: Kelsey 1 hour late for second shift.	*Johnson had to continue working after first shift ended.*

Identifying Desired Results

Remember, the purpose of giving feedback isn't to dwell on the past—it's to plan for the future. Can you identify and describe the results that

Leadership Series

you hope your reinforcement or redirection will produce? After you give your feedback, what types of actions do you hope to see?

In the case of reinforcement, the answer is easy—you hope to see the act in question repeated and developed. In the case of redirection, you may need to give a little more thought to this question. You will want to accept input from the person receiving your redirection about specific short- and long-term goals. But you should have some goals in mind. Keep these goals in sight as you talk to the person to ensure that the action plan you negotiate leads to the results *you* want.

Redirection should lead to the results you want.

Understanding Expectations

Does the person receiving the feedback understand your expectations for his or her behavior and job performance? This is an especially important question for cases of redirection. Often, we assume that people understand exactly what they are supposed to be doing in a given situation, but that may not be the case. Ask yourself what you (and others) have done in the past to clarify your expectations. Refer to the person's job description and to previous performance evaluations—have your expectations ever been addressed before?

Suppose you discover that no one has ever addressed the act in question with your feedback recipient. Then your redirection may take the form of clarifying your expectations. If the expectations are new to the staff member, you may also need to discuss such questions as:

- Are the expectations fair and reasonable?

- Is the feedback recipient capable of meeting them?

- Are there ways in which co-workers can help the feedback recipient meet the expectations?

Controlling the Situation

Is the person receiving the feedback really responsible for the act in question? The person to whom you are planning to give your feedback may have no trouble understanding your expectations yet be unable to meet them. This could occur for a variety of reasons. Perhaps the feedback recipient is not actually responsible for the situation you are addressing. Or, perhaps the recipient does not have the resources to redirect or repeat his or her actions.

Before you give feedback to anyone, try to discover if other people might be responsible for the situation. You may want to reinforce Ben's addition of bar graphs to the weekly population reports. But he can only do this when the shift supervisors give him the figures on time. Perhaps the shift supervisors need your reinforcement, too.

Suppose you think outside factors may be affecting your feedback recipient's actions, but you aren't sure. Ask the recipient in the course of giving your feedback. Then take his or her response into account as the two of you develop plans for the future.

Accepting Feedback

Is the other person open to accepting feedback from you? This will depend on your relationship with the person receiving your feedback and his or her attitude toward the feedback process. Questions to ask yourself include:

- Are you a credible feedback source for

this person? Does your feedback recipient believe that you have the expertise to provide competent redirection or reinforcement? If you believe your credibility may be an issue, make doubly sure you have plenty of examples to support your comments.

- Is your relationship with your feedback recipient cordial and professional? People are always willing to accept suggestions more readily from someone with whom they have a good working relationship. Suppose you do not have a good relationship with your receiver, or perhaps have criticized (rather than redirected) the receiver's work in the past. In this case, you may need to re-establish your relationship before your feedback can be effective.

- What is your status relative to the feedback recipient's? In hierarchical organizations, it is often difficult to give feedback, especially redirection, to a manager or supervisor. If you are presenting feedback to a higher-up, provide plenty of examples to establish your credibility. And remember to present your comments as supportive rather than critical.

Delaying Feedback

Delaying feedback makes it harder to give feedback.

Have you put off giving this feedback for a long time? If you previously looked on feedback as unpleasant or unimportant, you may have put off approaching the receiver with your feedback. Unfortunately, delaying feedback makes it harder to give that feedback when you finally do sit down with your receiver.

- If you have delayed giving redirection, the situation may have had time to escalate from a minor glitch to a serious problem.

- If you have delayed giving reinforcement, your recipient may not remember the act in question and may wonder why it has taken you so long to respond.

- The receiver of your feedback may not be open to your input after such a long delay. Delayed redirection can often result in responses like "But that's the way we've always done it" from the recipient.

You may need to explain to your feedback recipient that you realize your feedback is late or not on time. If you have been avoiding a feedback session, don't put it off any longer—Immediately schedule a session and start to prepare for it. Don't delay!

Taking Time for Feedback

Have you given yourself enough time to prepare your feedback? Don't kid yourself—it takes time to think about all of the issues we've just mentioned as well as to document the actions you hope to redirect or reinforce. Always give yourself enough time so that you begin every feedback session fully prepared.

Take a Moment . . .

Think of someone in your workplace to whom you need to give feedback about the quality of his or her efforts. Perhaps you need to redirect that person's performance. Perhaps there's a behavior that is inappropriate or unsatisfactory.

Use the Feedback Plan provided to help you prepare the necessary feedback. If you take the time to consider each of the questions, you should be fully prepared for the feedback session.

Feedback Plan

1. Do you think the person receiving the feedback understands your expectations for his or her behavior or performance?

   _____ Yes _____ No

   If no, how can you clarify your expectations? _____

   _____

   _____

2. Do you think the person receiving the feedback is really responsible for the behavior or performance in question?

   _____ Yes _____ No

   If no, who should be the target of the feedback? _____

   _____

   _____

3. Do you think the other person is open to receiving feedback from you?

   _____ Yes _____ No

   If no how can you re-establish your relationship? _____

   _____

   _____

4. Have you put off giving this feedback for a long time?

   _____ Yes _____ No

   If yes, how will you address the delay? _____

   _____

   _____

5. Have you given yourself enough time to prepare the feedback?

   _____ Yes _____ No

   If no, reschedule the feedback and give yourself more time to prepare.

Identify and accurately describe the specific actions you want to reinforce or redirect and their influence on others.

_____

_____

_____

_____

List detailed examples of these actions and their effects to use as support for Question #1.

_____

_____

_____

_____

Identify and describe the results that you hope your reinforcement or redirection will produce.

_____

_____

The next chapter will describe a series of steps that will guide you through the feedback process.

Chapter Three Review

Suggested answers appear on page 95.

1. **True/False.** You may find yourself putting more time into planning your feedback than you do actually giving it.

2. **True/False.** It isn't necessary to identify and describe specific actions that you want to redirect or reinforce—just stating that you like or dislike someone's work is enough.

3. **True/False.** You should always be sure that your feedback recipient understands your expectations for his or her performance before you begin a feedback session.

4. **True/False.** Before you begin a feedback session, you should be sure that the person you will be redirecting or reinforcing is actually responsible for the action in question.

5. **True/False.** Delayed feedback is no more difficult to give than timely feedback.

Chapter Four

STEPS FOR GIVING EFFECTIVE FEEDBACK

Chapter Objectives

After completing this chapter, you should be able to:

- Use the basic steps for reinforcing effective job performance and job-related behavior.

- Use the basic steps for redirecting ineffective job performance and job-related behavior.

- Describe how the amount of information you give your feedback recipient can help that person achieve individual, group, and organizational goals.

Preparing to Give Your Feedback

If you've done everything you can to plan your feedback, giving that feedback should be relatively easy. You can begin the process by choosing the time and place to present your feedback.

Choosing an Appropriate Time and Place

Try to give your feedback in a situation where you won't be distracted by other people or concerns. Plan ahead and make an appointment with your feedback recipient—choose a time when neither of you will be too tired or

. . . choose a time when neither of you will be too tired or stressed.

stressed.

If you are giving redirection, you will want to choose a private place where your conversation won't be overheard. If you are giving the same redirection to a group of people—such as instructing a group of correctional officers on a better way to conduct searches—you can present your comments to the entire group. However, under most circumstances, you should not redirect an individual in front of other staff.

Reinforcement can sometimes be given more informally. If your comments will be brief, you might ask the person to step inside your office for a moment rather than scheduling a formal appointment. If your organizational culture supports public recognition of staff, you can give reinforcement in front of others, such as during a weekly staff meeting. This can be an effective way of recognizing an accomplishment as well as demonstrating to other staff members the type of actions you want to reinforce.

Beginning the Feedback Session

Your demeanor or behavior sets the tone for the meeting.

Whether you are redirecting or reinforcing a staff member or co-worker, try to help that person feel comfortable as you begin the feedback session. If the feedback session is taking place in your office, invite the other person to sit down. If the other person seems especially nervous or uncomfortable, "break the ice" with some casual conversation before getting into your topic.

Your demeanor or behavior sets the tone for the meeting. As your feedback session progresses, keep your own emotions in check—especially if you are attempting to redirect a problem that has frustrated you in the past. Remain calm and keep your voice even throughout the session. Do not say or do anything that would cause the person receiving your feedback to become emotional. For example, do not shout at or berate a staff member.

Presenting Your Feedback

Once you have established a positive tone for the feedback session, the process should flow smoothly. Remember that your goal is to specify (give) as much detailed, useful information as possible to help the staff member or co-worker be as productive as possible. You can do that easily by following the basic steps for reinforcement and redirection.

Basic Steps for Giving Reinforcement

You can give reinforcement that staff members and co-workers will remember if you follow these four easy steps:

1. Describe the behavior or performance you want to reinforce.

2. Explain the positive influence the act has had on the organization.

3. Help your feedback recipient take credit for his or her success.

4. Thank your feedback recipient for his or her contribution toward meeting group or organizational goals (or meeting individual goals) and encourage similar future actions.

The steps for giving reinforcement are summarized in the following diagram.

Steps for Giving Reinforcement

Step 1
Describe the behavior
or performance
you want to reinforce.

Step 2
Explain the positive influence
that act has had on the
organization.

Step 3
Help your
feedback recipient
take credit for his
or her success.

Step 4
Thank your recipient
and encourage similar acts
in the future.

American Correctional Association

Step 1—Describe the Behavior or Performance You Want to Reinforce

You should begin any reinforcement session with a description of the behavior or performance you would like to reinforce. Remember, the purpose of giving reinforcement isn't just to make the other person feel good. It's to describe the act you want to reinforce in such a way that the person receiving the feedback will be able to repeat it. The more detail you give staff in the course of reinforcement, the better they will be able to repeat and build on their work. Consider these two sets of examples: Which responses do you think give the receivers of the feedback enough information to repeat their performance?

Example One

"Thanks for reorganizing the files, Cindy. They look great!"

"I'm very impressed with the way you've reorganized the files, Cindy. Organizing the files by dates makes them much easier to find, and I especially like the way you put the frequently used files on the bottom where we can all reach them."

Example Two

"Thanks for working overtime last night to proofread the report, Kurt. I hope it didn't keep you up too late."

"Thanks for the extra effort you put into proofreading the report this month, Kurt. I especially appreciate the time you took to check all of the totals and percentages—I noticed you caught several significant errors."

In each example, the receivers of the second response will know exactly what they should do they next time they perform these tasks.

Step 2—Explain the Behavior's Positive Influence

Most of us like to know how our efforts fit into the big picture. Learning how our work supports the work of others helps us to see our importance to the organization.

Explaining the positive influence a staff member's actions have had on the organization has two additional benefits. It can help the person see the *value* of his or her contribution, and it can create *extra incentive* to repeat and develop that act. Again, the more information you can give someone about the influence of his or her contribution, the more valuable your feedback will be. Consider the following example:

> *"I know that with so many staff out sick this month, it took extra effort for you to get the quarterly report out on time. Thanks to your efforts, management had the information they needed to make some important decisions about adding new staff; in fact, they approved the new staff we've been hoping for."*

The staff member receiving this reinforcement will know exactly how her hard work influenced her organization and her team.

. . . the more information you can give someone about the influence of his or her contribution, the more valuable your feedback will be.

Step 3—Help Your Feedback Recipient Take Credit for Success

"Oh, it was no big deal. I had a lot of help."

Although just about everyone craves positive reinforcement, it's amazing how many people have trouble
accepting it when it's given to them. Many of us were
raised with the attitude that accepting a compliment is similar to brag-
ging. Or, perhaps we just have a hard time believing that we can actually
do something right!

Help those you reinforce accept full responsibility for their success.
You can acknowledge the contributions of others if your feedback recipient mentions them. But emphasize the full importance of your recipient's
role:

"I realize that the entire committee was involved in making the open house a
success, but I want especially to thank you for all of your work arranging
transportation. Thanks to you, all of the participants arrived in plenty of time
to make their presentations."

Providing a strong example of a modest person's positive influence
is a good way to help her realize the significance of her efforts.

Step 4—Thank and Encourage Your Feedback Recipient

"Thank you" is still one of those magic expressions
we love to hear, so be sure to say "thanks" whenever
you present reinforcement. Include your thanks at the
end of your reinforcement, after you have described the
act and its influence. This way, it will be the last thing
the staff member takes away from the interaction.

Make sure that your feedback recipient knows you hope to see the
positive behavior or performance repeated in similar situations. As
you thank your feedback recipient, encourage him or her to keep up the
good work.

Take a Moment . . .

Think of someone you work with whose positive behavior or performance you would like to reinforce. With that individual in mind, decide what you intend to say at each step of the process.

Describe the behavior or performance you want to reinforce.

_____

_____

_____

Explain the positive influence the behavior or performance has had on the organization.

_____

_____

_____

Help your feedback recipient take responsibility for his or her success.

_____

_____

_____

Thank your feedback recipient for his or her contribution toward meeting individual or organizational goals (or meeting individual goals), and encourage similar future behavior or performance.

_____

_____

_____

Basic Steps for Giving Redirection

Redirection consists of six basic steps that will help your feedback recipient see the influence of his or her acts and plan for the future:

1. Describe the behavior or performance you want to redirect.

2. Listen to the reaction of your feedback recipient. Your feedback recipient may immediately admit there is a problem and take responsibility for it. If so, you're at step 4 and proceed from there. If not, you may need to go to Step 3.

3. Clarify your expectations for your feedback recipient's behavior or performance (3a). Or, explain the negative influence those actions are having on the organization (3b).

4. Help your feedback recipient to acknowledge that a problem exists and take responsibility for it. If he or she is unclear about your expectations, go back again to step 3a. If he or she refuses to take responsibility for the problem, go back to step 3b. Then proceed to step 4. Once you have agreed that there is a problem and the feedback recipient is willing to take responsibility for it, proceed to step 5. Note: Without this agreement, you will not see a long-term change in behavior or performance.

5. Develop a plan that will help your feedback recipient adjust his or her actions.

6. Thank your feedback recipient for his or her efforts.

The steps for giving redirection are summarized in the following diagram.

Leadership Series

6 Steps for Giving Redirection

1 Describe

Describe behavior or performance
you want to redirect.

2 Listen

Listen to recipient's
reaction.

| *Recipient confused about expectations.* *Go to step 3a.* | *Recipient agrees there is a problem.* *Go to step 4* | *Recipient unwilling to accept responsibility.* *Go to step 3b.* |

3a Clarify

Clarify expectations for
recipient's behavior or
performance.

3b Explain

Explain negative
influence of
recipient's actions.

4 Help

Help recipient
to acknowledge problem
and take responsibility for it.

Return to step 3a or 3b if necessary.

5 Develop

Develop a plan for future action.

6 Thank

Thank your feedback recipient.

Steps for Giving Redirection

Step 1—Describe the Behavior or Performance You Want to Redirect

Once again, you should begin the feedback session with a description of the behavior or performance you want to redirect. If the act you are describing is ongoing, try to cite more than one instance of it. This way, your feedback recipient can get an idea of the extent of the problem.

Behavior in need of redirection:
"Bob, you were late to work three times this week and twice last week. You were also late five times last month."

Describe behavior or performance you want to redirect.

Performance in need of redirection:
"Martha, I found five errors in this report you just finished, and you misspelled the inmate's name. I also found several errors in the last two reports you did."

In both examples, the person giving the feedback simply described the behavior or performance in question without making a value judgment or expressing anger or disappointment. Beginning your feedback this way will keep your redirection focused on acts or behaviors rather than attitudes.

Step 2—Listen to the Reaction of Your Feedback Recipient

2

Listen to recipient's reaction.

Once you have given a detailed description of the behavior or performance you hope to change, give your feedback recipient a chance to respond. Three responses feedback recipients often give are:

- acknowledging the problem

- expressing confusion over expectations

- refusing to accept responsibility

Acknowledging the Problem. Often, staff are aware of a problem and have been waiting for an opportunity to discuss it:

> *"I know the formatting on the reports has been difficult to read. I've been trying to use the new software, but I just can't figure out how to do it. Can someone show me how?"*

If you receive a response like this, it shows that your feedback recipient has taken responsibility for the problem and is ready to correct it. Congratulations, there is no need for Step 3. You have proceeded to and completed Step 4! No further discussion of your staff member's or co-worker's actions are necessary. The two of you can immediately begin to develop an action plan to correct the problem, which is described in Step 5.

Expressing Confusion. Of course, not all feedback sessions will resolve so quickly. Your feedback recipient may respond with confusion about your expectations. Perhaps your staff member or co-worker never understood (or was not given) a clear description of his or her job duties. Or, perhaps expectations for the job have changed over time.

"I didn't realize that I was supposed to provide the figures by the beginning of the month—I thought that any time during the first week would be fine."

When you receive a response like this, you should clarify expectations with your feedback recipient, which we will describe in Step 3a.

Refusing to Accept Responsibility. Occasionally your feedback recipient may admit that a problem exists but refuse to take responsibility for it. We've all heard (and possibly given) responses like:

"It's not my fault! It's the other people on the shift."

"I'll try to do better, but you know, there just isn't enough time."

In situations like these, your challenge is to determine whether some outside factor is affecting your feedback recipient's ability to do the job— or whether he or she is just making excuses. This is especially difficult if your staff member or co-worker is behaving defensively.

Try to get past your feedback recipient's defensiveness and focus on the content of what he or she is saying. If factors within the organization or work team are keeping him or her from meeting your expectations, use this time to address them. As staff members and co-workers see that you take their viewpoints seriously, their responses will become less defensive and more cooperative.

Of course, there also will be times when you listen to someone's explanation and determine that you must hold that person responsible for the problem. If your feedback recipient remains defensive and refuses to take responsibility for the problem, focus the conversation on the influence of his or her actions (as we will discuss in Step 3b). This is your best evidence that the problem falls on the recipient.

3a

Clarify expectations for recipient's behavior or performance.

Step 3a—Clarify Your Expectations

If your feedback recipient is surprised or confused by the expectations you have for his or her performance, take the time to clarify them. This might involve referring back to the original job description or reviewing the directions your recipient has received for performing certain tasks.

As you review your expectations, be sure to give the staff member or co-worker plenty of opportunity to respond. Be sure that your feedback recipient agrees that the expectations are reasonable. If he or she doesn't agree, you may need to point out that other people in the organization are working just as hard. Or, you may need to readjust your expectations in some way. Whatever you negotiate, by the end of this step:

• you and your feedback recipient should agree on a set of reasonable expectations

• your feedback recipient should be ready to acknowledge his or her responsibility for meeting them

You can develop this further in Step 4.

Step 3b—Explain the Action's Negative Influence

You can help a defensive feedback recipient recognize the need to redirect his or her actions. The best way to achieve this goal is by giving a thorough description of the influence those actions are having on other staff. Again, you should simply state the facts without expressing anger or making a value judgment. Here are two examples based on descriptions we used earlier:

"When you're late, other staff have to fill in for you until you arrive. Joe had to work overtime twice this week until you arrived, and Sara had to cover for you last week. It isn't fair to the others to expect them to cover for you, and it hurts the quality of our work to keep tired employees on duty after their shift is over."

"When we process reports with errors, it looks as though we don't care about our work. It encourages people to think that government workers always do substandard work."

Descriptions like these should help your feedback recipient see the influence of his behavior or performance and take responsibility for adjusting his behavior. If your recipient is especially defensive, keep returning to your examples—until he is ready to accept responsibility and work out a plan to foster change.

3b

Explain negative influence of recipient's actions.

Step 4—Help Your Recipient Acknowledge That a Problem Exists and Take Responsibility for It

4

Help recipient to acknowledge problem and take responsibility for it.

If you can get people to recognize the negative consequences or influences of something they are doing, they will usually agree that it is a problem.

You and your feedback recipient cannot collaborate in redirecting behavior or performance until he acknowledges that a problem exists and takes responsibility for correcting it. You will know that you have this agreement when you hear your feedback recipient say something like, "Yes, I agree, there's a problem. But what can I do about it?"

Suppose your feedback recipient is slow to acknowledge the problem and accept responsibility. In this case, you should to back to 3a and clarify your expectations. Or, you should go back to Step 3b and continue to present evidence about the extent of the problem until you have agreement. What kind of evidence can you use to convince your recipient that a problem exists and that his or her behavior or performance needs to change?

- Stress the negative influence that the individual's current performance or behavior is having on co-workers and the organization as a whole.

- Convince the individual that he or she will face significant consequences if the behavior or performance continues.

If you can get people to recognize the negative consequences or influences of something they are doing, they will usually agree that it is a problem.

Step 5—Develop an Action Plan

The goal of any redirection is improving future performance and behavior. It isn't enough just to point out the need for change to your feedback recipient—you also need to develop a specific plan to help him or her set and meet goals. A goal is something to aim for, something you want to achieve. It's a clear statement of the behavior you want.

Develop a plan for future action.

You should have some short- and long-term goals in mind before you begin your feedback session. But you will want to involve your feedback recipient in the planning process. One way you can do this is by stating an overall goal and then asking for the staff member's input on how to meet that goal. Here is an example in which an administrative assistant redirects her manager's difficulty with meeting deadlines:

Administrative Assistant: *"I really want to get letters and reports typed on time. But I have difficulty when you give me your tapes to transcribe a half hour before the mail has to go out. Is there some way you can give me more time?"*

Manager: *"It's difficult. Those are open cases, and I often don't have the information I need until the last minute."*

Administrative Assistant: *"Well, could you let me know at the beginning of the day if you think you'll need me to transcribe something? That way, I could organize my work so that my last hour is free for your projects."*

Manager: *"I think I can do that."*

The administrative assistant might not have gotten as much time for her transcription as she would have liked. But she was able to involve her manager in a solution that would help her organize her time effectively, which was her primary goal. When the manager remembers to tell the assistant about an upcoming transcription, the assistant can reinforce the action by saying something like "Thanks for telling me so early. I can get much more done when I have the opportunity to organize my day in advance."

Step 6—Thank Your Feedback Recipient for His or Her Efforts

6

Thank your feedback recipient.

It can be hard to accept redirection. Show your feedback recipient that you appreciate his or her efforts by closing your redirection with a "Thank you." This can also be a good time to summarize your conversation and make plans for future meetings:

"Thanks for taking the time to talk to me about the reports. I really appreciate your willingness to arrange your time to meet our deadlines, and I want to help you any way I can. Let's meet again next week to see how things are going for you."

Stay on Track

These steps for giving reinforcement and redirection will allow you to give useful, supportive feedback that focuses on acts or behaviors rather than attitudes. Following these steps should get you through even a potentially difficult feedback situation with a minimum of stress. But the steps can help you only if you follow them. Think of them as a road or pathway. Stay headed in the right direction. Don't allow yourself to get distracted in the course of a feedback session and turn onto a different road. Even if your feedback recipient tries to steer the conversation onto other topics or becomes argumentative, focus on the steps. They will give your feedback session direction and ensure that you provide your recipient with as much useful information as possible.

Take a Moment . . .

Think of someone you work with whose behavior or performance you would like to redirect. With that individual in mind, decide what you intend to say at each step of the process.

Describe the behavior or performance you want to redirect.

_____

_____

_____

Imagine what you think that person's response might be.

_____

_____

_____

Clarify your expectations for your feedback receiver. Or, explain the negative influence the behavior or performance has had on the organization and help your receiver take responsibility for his or her actions.

_____

_____

Help your recipient to acknowledge that a problem exists and take responsibility for it.

_____

_____

Develop a plan that will help the receiver of your feedback adjust his or her actions or behavior.

_____

_____

Thank your feedback recipient.

_____

Document Your Feedback

Too often, we're so busy handling day-to-day worries that we forget to make note of the positive things we encounter. When you give a staff member or co-worker reinforcement on a significant achievement or project, don't forget to document your feedback for that individual's personnel file. Making a record of your positive assessment will help the staff member receive the rewards and recognition he or she deserves in the evaluation process.

You also should make note of any redirection that you give. Even if you do not think that the problem is serious enough to include in a personnel file, keep a record of the redirection for yourself. Include the types of details we discussed in Chapter Three—these are the key elements of good documentation:

- What happened?

- Where and when did it occur?

- Who was involved?

- How did it affect others?

- What was the outcome?

If the staff member successfully redirects his performance, you will have a record of the feedback process that will help you track his success. And, if he does not respond to redirection and the problem becomes worse, you will have documentation that you attempted to deal with it. This could be significant if the problem becomes so serious that the staff member must be disciplined or terminated.

Providing Higher Levels of Information

In Chapter Two, we discussed the process of specifying—providing more and more specific, detailed information to your feedback recipient. Following the steps for redirection (or reinforcement) that we've discussed will help you provide the detailed information your feedback receiver needs to meet individual and organizational goals. Each step of the feedback process provides further details that can help your feedback recipient improve his or her performance or behavior.

ACHIEVING GOALS

Amount of
Detailed
Information

Specifying details

Probing for details

Giving Feedback

Receiving Feedback

Giving Feedback—Redirection

Step 1. Describe behavior/performance
Step 2. Listen to response
Step 3. Clarify expectations/explain negative
       influence
Step 4. Acknowledge problem and take
       responsibility
Step 5. Develop action plan
Step 6. Thank recipient

**Redirection = More information =
More help in achieving goals**

Chapter Four Review

Suggested answers appear on pages 95 and 96.

1. **True/False.** There is no need to worry about scheduling an appropriate time for giving feedback. You can provide redirection and reinforcement anytime, anywhere.

2. **True/False.** It is perfectly all right to redirect an individual staff member in the presence of other staff members. It shows you're in charge and expect a certain level of performance.

3. List the four basic steps for providing reinforcement.

_____

_____

_____

_____

4. List the six basic steps for providing redirection.

_____

_____

_____

_____

_____

_____

5. **True/False.** It is important to document both reinforcement and redirection.

Chapter Five

STEPS FOR RECEIVING FEEDBACK EFFECTIVELY

Chapter Objectives

After completing this chapter, you should be able to:

- Use the basic steps for receiving reinforcement or redirection of your job performance and job-related behavior.

- Probe for more information when receiving redirection or reinforcement.

- Describe how the amount of information you receive can help you achieve individual, team and organizational goals.

How Do You Respond to Feedback?

Think about the last time you received feedback from someone. What did you do? Did you listen to the feedback and try to learn as much as you could from it? Did you ask questions in order to receive as much detailed information as possible? Or did you become defensive?

It's always tempting to make excuses whenever we receive redirection. After all, you probably had very good reasons for approaching your work the way you did, and it's natural to want to explain those reasons. But if you spend all your time explaining yourself, you won't have time to really hear what the person giving redirection is trying to say—that your actions are creating some negative results for your organization and need to be changed. You must put aside your feelings of defensiveness to be able to focus on the details that can help you change your behavior or performance.

You can make the same kind of mistake when you receive reinforcement. If someone compliments your work, you may want to stop right there and enjoy the praise without asking for further details. Or, if you're a modest person, you may want to deny the praise completely. You won't benefit from either approach. There is only one way you will be able to repeat your actions and develop them further. You must probe for specific details about what aspects of your behavior or performance have had the most positive results and how you should repeat them.

Take a Moment . . .

Think about the last time you received redirection from someone. What did you do?

_____

_____

_____

Is this typical of how you respond to redirection?

Think about how you usually respond to feedback. Do you tend to: (Check all that apply.)

___Get defensive and try to explain your actions?

___Shut down and not listen, focusing instead on what you're going to say to defend yourself?

___Find someone with whom to share all or part of the blame for the problem?

___Shut down and not listen, focusing instead on what you can do to regain favor in the other person's eyes?

___Listen carefully to what the person is saying so that you can understand and probe for more information, if necessary?

Think about the last time you received reinforcement from someone. What did you do?

_____

_____

_____

Is this typical of how you respond to reinforcement?

Think about how you usually respond to reinforcement. Do you tend to: (Check all that apply.)

___Deny the praise?

___Shut down and not listen, focusing instead on what you're going to say to deny the praise?

___Find someone with whom to share all or part of the praise?

___Shut down and not listen, focusing instead on what you can do to shift the conversation away from the praise?

___Listen carefully to what the person is saying so that you can understand and probe for more information, if necessary?

Listen and Learn from Feedback

You'll get the most from redirection and reinforcement if you make the commitment to *listen* and *learn* in all feedback situations. Listening and learning well will require you to develop the following habits.

- Become a careful listener.

- Keep all feedback in perspective.

- Try to learn from all feedback, even feedback that is presented poorly.

Become a Careful Listener

The first thing you can do to get the most from every feedback session is to develop effective listening skills. Listening is probably the most important communication skill we can develop, yet few of us know how to listen effectively. How many times have you found your mind wandering when someone was talking to you? Any distracting thoughts can keep a person from being an effective listener, an impending deadline, rumors about staff changes—even worries about a child's Little League game.

It's especially easy for us to become distracted when we are receiving feedback. We listen with all of the other concerns that generally crowd our minds for attention. We also may be trying to generate excuses for our acts even as they are being described to us.

Try to enter every feedback situation with the attitude that you will concentrate on what the person giving feedback is saying. Don't try to generate responses as the person is talking, just listen. If the person's viewpoint seems strange to you, ask yourself why he or she might see things in that way. You will likely have plenty of time to present your own observations after he or she is done talking.

Keep Feedback in Perspective

It's easy to overreact to feedback. If someone reinforces our positive behavior or successful performance, it's natural to enjoy the positive feelings of knowing that we have done our job well. But we must avoid extending that positive reaction to the point that we believe we can do no wrong. To do so, we would be creating an unrealistic view of our own abilities.

The same thing can happen when we receive redirection, especially if that redirection is given in an inappropriate or overly critical manner. (Remember, not everyone has the expertise you will be able to demonstrate when you complete this workbook.) By dwelling on the negative, you can turn a simple comment on one specific act into a criticism of your entire job performance—or even your life!

Remember to keep all feedback in perspective. Use feedback as a *guide* to determine whether you should repeat or change specific actions, not as something to dwell on.

Try to Learn from All Feedback

In a perfect world, all of the feedback we receive would be presented in an appropriate manner. If your organization is encouraging all of its staff to give each other useful, ongoing feedback, this is certainly the goal. However, human beings aren't perfect, and feedback is sometimes given poorly even in the most well-intentioned organizations. It's tempting to write off inappropriate feedback as rude and obnoxious. But by doing so, you may miss out on important information that can help you do your job better.

As you become more experienced in receiving feedback, you will be able to exert some control in situations where feedback is given to you ineffectively. By asking appropriate questions, you can salvage many feedback situations that get off on the wrong foot and gain valuable information in the process. You also will help other staff develop effective feedback skills by modeling those skills and encouraging them to do so in return.

Remember, make a commitment to attempt to learn something from all feedback you receive, even in situations that initially seem unpleasant.

Take A Moment . . .

Describe a situation in which you were given feedback poorly.

_____

_____

_____

Separate the poor behavior from the message. Was there something you could learn from the feedback that can improve your behavior? If so, identify it.

_____

_____

Are You Ready for Feedback?

You've made the commitment to listen to both redirection and reinforcement with an open mind and to avoid denying or making excuses for what you hear. Are you ready for the next feedback session? Not yet. You'll be ready when you can help ensure an effective feedback process. You can do this by:

- Helping choose the appropriate time and place

- Staying calm, cordial and professional

- Asking questions

Help Choose the Appropriate Time and Place

Has the person giving you feedback asked for your help in choosing an appropriate time and place? If so, help him or her create a situation in which neither of you will be distracted or uncomfortable.

If you're not asked about the time or place, you do still have options. Suppose someone begins to give you feedback in an inappropriate setting—providing redirection in a busy hallway or in front of a group of co-workers or offenders, for example. Politely ask if you can move the discussion to another time and place where you can give it your full attention. Suppose you find yourself in a situation in which you believe you are being belittled in front of others. You are perfectly within your rights to ask that the topic be taken up in another setting.

Stay Calm, Cordial and Professional

Approach every feedback situation with confidence, knowing that the information you receive will help you improve your performance and move closer toward your goals. Resolve to stay calm, use a pleasant tone of voice, and maintain eye contact throughout the interaction. Even if the person giving feedback becomes unpleasant, it doesn't help the situation if you raise your voice. Remain cordial and professional.

Don't Be Afraid to Ask Questions

The more detailed information you receive in the course of a feedback session, the more that feedback session will benefit you. The way to guarantee that you receive useful redirection or reinforcement is to ask questions—to probe for more and more details and to be sure that you understand those details. We will discuss the process for receiving feedback in the next several pages.

Basic Steps for Receiving Feedback

The process of probing for information can be easy if you follow these steps:

- Ask for as much detailed information as possible.
- Paraphrase what you think you've heard.
- Seek suggestions for future action.
- Thank the person giving the feedback.

The steps for receiving feedback are summarized below.

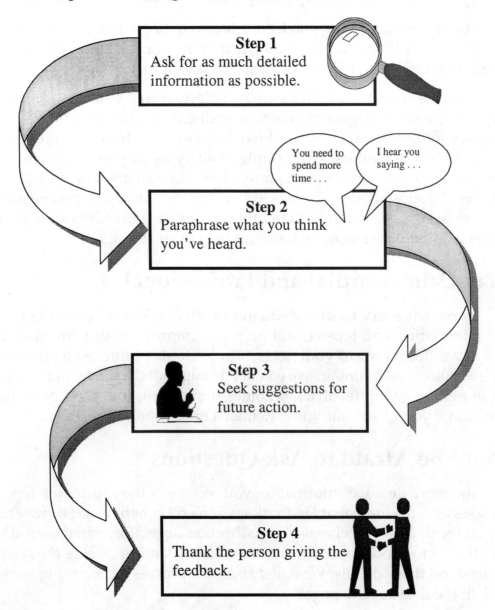

Step 1
Ask for as much detailed information as possible.

You need to spend more time . . .

I hear you saying . . .

Step 2
Paraphrase what you think you've heard.

Step 3
Seek suggestions for future action.

Step 4
Thank the person giving the feedback.

Step 1—Ask for Details

Whether you are receiving reinforcement or redirection, it's important to probe for as many details as possible. Sometimes probing may be as easy as thanking someone for a compliment:

"I'm so glad you liked the work I did on the year-end report to the state." If you tell me specifically what it was you liked about it, I'll be able to do it again on the next one."

In cases of redirection, probing may be a bit more difficult. You may not be eager to ask for examples of ways your actions have negatively influenced others. But it is worth the effort to probe for as many details as you can get—they are the tools you use to improve your performance and meet your goals. If the person you are addressing is skilled at giving feedback, you'll find it easy to get as much information as you need:

Manager: *"I never realized that my instructions to the word processing staff weren't clear. What information do you need from me that I'm not giving you?"*

Administrative Assistant: *"We really need you to tell us exactly when you need your project done instead of just saying "sometime soon," and we also need to know how many copies you want made for your files."*

Asking for more information is useful even when the person giving you feedback is not skilled at expressing himself or herself. Believe it or not, requesting details is one of the best ways to handle inappropriate feedback.

Consider this example:

Operations Manager: *"I don't know what the matter is with you people. Can't you do a simple* *shift schedule? "*

Shift Supervisor: *"I'm sorry you don't like this schedule. What don't you like about it?"*

Operations Manager: *"Well, it's awful, that's all!"*

Shift Supervisor: *"Let me start from the beginning. Do you dislike the assignments?"*

Operations Manager: *"No. They're fine."*

Shift Supervisor: *"Perhaps you don't like the chart format. Is that it?"*

Operations Manager: *"No. That's okay."*

Shift Supervisor: *"How about the order—do you want it set up differently?"*

Operations Manager: *"No. That's not it either. It's just too crowded—it looks all jumbled, and it's too hard to read."*

Shift Supervisor: *"So you think it needs more white space?"*

Operations Manager: *"Yes, that's it, white space and larger type—by the time this is copied, it's too hard to read."*

The Operations Manager in this example was not giving effective feedback—which forced the Shift Supervisor to work twice as hard to learn what was wrong with the schedule. The Shift Supervisor could easily have become frustrated with the Operations Manager, and the entire feedback session could have ended as a nasty argument. But by staying cool and asking for details, the Shift Supervisor was able to learn exactly what was bothering the Operations Manager. The supervisor can now use that information when preparing other schedules. Though the shift supervisor had to work a little to get the necessary information, the information gained will be worth the effort.

Do you work with someone who frequently gives you inappropriate feedback? You should consider giving that person some redirection on the way he or she is interacting with you. It is possible to comment on the way the person gives you feedback in a way that is constructive and nonthreatening. The Shift Supervisor in the first example might tell the Operations Manager something like this:

> *"I want to do schedules we both think are useful, but I can't really make the changes you want when your comments are so general. I think it would help both of us work better together if you would refer to specific parts of the schedules when you want me to make changes."*

Take A Moment . . .

Think of a situation in which you received general feedback, such as "Your searches are poor," or "Your interactions with the offender need work." Describe the situation.

_____

_____

_____

_____

What could you have said in a constructive or nonthreatening way to the person to get more specific feedback?

_____

_____

_____

Step 2—Paraphrase What You Think You Heard

Even with careful listening, you might miss some of the details of the feedback being presented to you. It's easy to focus in on just one aspect of the feedback and ignore the rest—especially if you are having a strong emotional reaction to what's being said. Paraphrasing your understanding of the feedback is a good way to make sure that your interpretation matches the intention of the person giving the feedback.

Wait until the other person has finished describing his perspective on the situation before you begin to paraphrase. Then simply restate your understanding of the feedback in your own words and ask the person giving the feedback if the interpretation is correct. Give the other person a chance to respond to your paraphrase and ask or add any additional information, if necessary.

Staff Member:

"So, what I hear you saying is that I need to spend a little more time with the inmates during their intake sessions."

Supervisor:

"That's right. They need to have a better understanding of our policies, and we need more information to place them in programs."

Step 3—Seek Suggestions for Future Action

Whether you're receiving reinforcement or redirection, feedback should never be a means to dwell on past performance. The purpose of feedback is to share information that will help you plan for the future.

Always be sure that future plans are discussed in the course of any feedback session. If you are receiving reinforcement, clarify exactly which acts should be repeated and when you should repeat them:

"I'm glad you like the way I handled the presentation in this morning's meeting. If you could tell me what you think were the strongest points, I'll be sure to do something similar in my next presentation."

If you are receiving redirection, ask the other person to help you develop a plan for changing your future actions.

"I realize I lost my temper when that correctional officer complained last week. I really don't know how to deal with them when they get so irate over their schedules. Do you have any suggestions?"

Never leave a feedback session until both you and the person giving the feedback have agreed on a future course of action.

Leadership Series

Step 4—Thank the Person Giving the Feedback

It takes courage to give another person direct, honest feedback. You should express that you value the effort the person made, including the time it took to prepare and present the feedback. Saying "Thank you" at the end of any feedback session will achieve this goal.

Though you may find it difficult, it's especially important to thank someone who has given you feedback in an ineffective way—especially because you probably were able to turn the interaction into a positive one by probing for useful information. Your handling of the situation has given the person the opportunity to learn more effective feedback techniques by observing how you probed for information. Saying "thanks" demonstrates that your behavior always remains professional and sets a positive tone for your next interaction.

Take a Moment . . .

Think of the last time someone gave you feedback that was lacking in specific details. What was the essence or basic message of the feedback you got?

_____

_____

_____

What could you have said to the person to probe for more information?

What details might you have asked for?

_____

_____

How might you have paraphrased his or her words?

_____

_____

How might you have sought suggestions for future action?

_____

_____

What could you have said to acknowledge the person giving the feedback?

_____

_____

Probing for Higher Levels of Information

In Chapter Four, we learned that a person giving feedback can use the process of specifying to provide increasing amounts of information—information that will help the feedback receiver achieve his or her goals. The process of probing has the same result.

As the person receiving feedback follows the steps of asking for information, he or she receives more and more specific details about job performance. The diagram below shows how this works. The more details you are able to receive from a feedback situation, the more tools you

ACHIEVING GOALS

Amount of Detailed Information

Specifying details

Giving Feedback

Probing for details

Receiving Feedback

Giving Feedback—Redirection

Step 1. Ask for detailed information.
Step 2. Paraphrase what you think you've heard.
Step 3. Seek suggestions for future action.
Step 4. Thank the person giving feedback.

**Asking for more information =
Receiving more details =
Receiving more help for achieving your
personal and work goals**

have to help you achieve greater and greater success.

By following the steps for giving and receiving feedback effectively, you (and your co-workers) can share information about job performance and behaviors easily. In our next chapter, you will have the chance to see what role your individual communication style plays in the feedback process.

Chapter Five Review

Suggested answers appear on page 96 and 97.

1. **True/False.** Even with the right attitude, you can only learn from an appropriate or good feedback situation.

2. **True/False.** You should try to keep all feedback in perspective; don't allow the redirection of one act to cause you to question your entire job performance.

3. **True/False.** Suppose a person begins to give you feedback at an inappropriate time and place. You should politely ask him or her if you can find a better setting where neither of you will be distracted.

4. **True/False.** Eye contact with the person giving you feedback really isn't important. If you feel uncomfortable during a feedback session, just look at the floor or the wall.

5. List the four basic steps for effectively receiving feedback.

   _____

   _____

   _____

   _____

6. **True/False.** Remaining calm and asking for further details is an effective way to deal with someone who is giving you inappropriate feedback.

7. **True/False.** Always remember to thank a person who has just given you feedback, even if the interaction started off on the wrong foot.

Chapter Six

FEEDBACK AND COMMUNICATION STYLES

Chapter Objectives

After completing this chapter, you should be able to:

- Identify your preferred communication style.

- Describe the influence your preferred communication style has on the way you tend to give and receive feedback.

- Describe other styles of communication and how those styles relate to feedback.

- Adapt your communication style to the needs of the feedback situation, particularly the needs of feedback recipients.

What Are Communication Styles?

Communication styles play an important part in the giving and receiving of feedback. All of us have developed communication patterns that reflect our individual identities. These patterns develop over time and become our preferred way of communicating.

You can give and receive feedback more effectively if you are aware of your preferred communication style—as well as the preferred communication style of your feedback recipient or giver. By recognizing the strengths and weaknesses of both styles, you can more easily adjust your style to avoid conflicts and ensure understanding or smooth communication.

There are four major communication styles:

- **Driver**—The driver is direct and task-oriented.
- **Collaborator**—The collaborator is enthusiastic and relationship-oriented.
- **Contributor**—The contributor is supportive and avoids change and confrontation.
- **Investigator**—The investigator is accurate and detail-oriented.

Our communication styles usually include parts from each style. But the parts of one style usually dominate. The chart below describes some of the strengths and potential stumbling blocks associated with the four styles.

Communication Style	Strengths	Potential Stumbling Blocks
Driver	• Direct • Practical • Decisive • Confident • Clear, to the point • Task-oriented	• Challenge others • Impatient • Insensitive • Overly independent • Need for control, domineering • Inflexible
Collaborator	• Talkative • Friendly • Enthusiastic • Approachable, open • Initiates through involvement of others	• Overly sensitive • Lack of follow-through/details • Unprepared, disorganized • Subjective in decision-making • Hesitant to take a leadership role
Contributor	• Supportive, patient • Predictable • Easygoing, calm • Listens actively • Responsive to others	• Avoids confrontation, passive • Slow to change • Slow to initiate • Indecisive • Withholds feelings
Investigator	• Accurate, well-prepared • Diplomatic • Analytical • Cautious, restrained • Systematic, detail-oriented	• Too critical, insnsitive • Inflexible • Withdrawn • Overly cautious • Establishes unattainable standards

Take A Moment . . .

You

Which style comes closest to describing the way you tend to communicate?

_____

If you have trouble deciding, ask yourself which parts describe the way you *tend* to communicate?

_____

_____

_____

_____

_____

Which style does the *greatest number* of parts fall under?

_____

Your Supervisor

Which style comes closest to describing the way your supervisor tends to communicate?

_____

If you have trouble deciding, ask yourself which parts describe the way your supervisor *tends* to communicate?

_____

_____

_____

_____

_____

Which style does the *greatest number* of parts fall under?

_____

How Styles Affect Feedback

Most of us give and receive feedback in a manner consistent with our dominant communication style. Review the preferred way for giving and receiving feedback for each of the four styles, paying particular attention to your own style—as well as what you perceive your supervisor's to be.

Communication Style	Prefers to Give/Receive Feedback
Driver	• Quickly • Directly • To the point • Focusing on the "Whats"
Collaborator	• Conversationally • Allowing time for anecdotal support (examples, stories) • Sensitively • Allowing time for much verbalizing • Focusing on the "Whats"
Contributor	• Patiently, allowing time to respond • Nonthreateningly • Clearly • Supportively • Privately • Focusing on "Whats" and "Hows"
Investigator	• Objectively • Thoroughly • Accurately • Patiently, allowing time to change • With no surprises • Focusing on the "Whats" and "Whys"

Understanding the Communication Style of Others

Knowing and understanding your preferred communication style is important because in order to fully appreciate others' styles, you must first appreciate your own. You should be conscious of your own communication preferences when giving and receiving feedback from others. But your primary focus needs to be on what you believe the other person's preferences are.

If you are *giving* feedback to a co-worker or a staff member, you need to be sensitive to that person's communication style. Match that individual's style, or deliver your feedback in a way that is comfortable to the person. This way, he will be more likely to hear what you have to say and to be open to changing his behavior or improving his performance.

When *receiving* feedback from others, be aware of their preferred communication styles. Their styles tell you how they give feedback. Understanding their approach enables you to get beyond "how" they are giving you the feedback and enables you to concentrate on probing for specifics—the "whats" and "whys."

Let's look at an example of a supervisor with a Driver communication style redirecting the performance of a staff member with an Investigator style. Note how the supervisor adapts the basic steps for giving redirection to a style that is compatible with her staff member's style, not necessarily her own. She enters the feedback discussion well prepared, ready to provide lots of facts and specific details. She knows her staff member is going to want to know "why" he needs to improve his performance—not just "what" she sees as unsatisfactory performance.

"Driver" Giving Redirection to an "Investigator"

Step 1—Describe the behavior or performance you want to redirect.

Sharon: *"Garrett, we need to talk about your follow-through on the inmate inquiries assigned to you in the database. Over 50% have had initial contact but little follow-up."*

Step 2—Listen to the reaction of your feedback recipient.

Suppose Garrett acknowledges that he has not consistently followed through on inmate inquiries and that this is a problem. Sharon then can move immediately to Step 5 and help Garrett develop an action plan. Otherwise, Sharon must take the time to help Garrett understand and acknowledge the influence his performance is having on others. Until Garrett recognizes the consequences of his performance and takes responsibility for them, there's little incentive for him to change.

Step 3—Explain the influence the behavior/performance is having on the organization.

Sharon: *"When you are slow in following up on inquiries, it has far-reaching effects. We know that delays in follow-through result in more problems and more inquiries from the court. We need to respond to inmate inquiries faster to avoid compounding the problems. Our good record in the past has been really helpful in our work with the court. So we need to get back on track."*

Step 4—Help your feedback recipient acknowledge that a problem exists and take responsibility for it.

Sharon should continue to discuss the situation with Garrett until he acknowledges his responsibility for the situation:

Garrett: *"I can see that I need to move more quickly if I want to meet our performance goals. Let's set up a timetable."*

Step 5—Develop a plan that will help the receiver of your feedback adjust his or her actions.

Sharon: *"Garrett, in order to meet our goals, we need to reach resolution on all inquiries within four weeks of the inquiry date. What can you do, and how can I help, to increase your rate of follow-through?"*

Garrett and Sharon can now work together to:

* Set short- and long-term goals for Garrett's performance.

- Create an action plan that will help Garrett meet those goals.

Step 6—Thank your feedback recipient for his or her efforts.

After they've made specific plans, Sharon can thank Garrett, review their conversation, and arrange a future meeting:

Sharon: *"Garrett, thanks for taking the time for this talk. You've acknowledged that your delays in following up on inquiries are having negative effects, and you've identified several steps that will help you follow up more quickly. I'm here to help you if you need it. Let's get together again next Tuesday and assess the progress you've made."*

Take a Moment . . .

How well did Sharon (A Driver) do in matching the way she provided feedback to Garrett (An Investigator)?

Was she well prepared?	__Yes __No
Was she thorough?	__Yes __No
Did she explain the "Whys" for improving?	__Yes __No
Was she objective and nonaccusatory?	__Yes __No
Was she detailed and specific in her examples?	__Yes __No

Adjusting your feedback to the style of the person to whom you are speaking can help you give and receive feedback more effectively. In Chapter 7, you will have the chance to assess your current level of feedback skills and create an action plan for developing them further.

Chapter Six Review

Suggested answers appear on page 97.

1. Match each communication style with the appropriate description.
    A. Detail-oriented, accurate
    B. Direct, task-oriented
    C. Supportive, avoids change and confrontation
    D. Relationship-oriented, enthusiastic

    _____1. Collaborator

    _____2. Investigator

    _____3. Contributor

    _____4. Driver

2. To fully appreciate others' communication styles, what must you do?

    _____

    _____

    _____

    _____

    _____

3. What should you be aware of and match when giving or receiving feedback?

    _____

    _____

    _____

    _____

    _____

Chapter Seven

HANDLING DIFFICULT FEEDBACK SITUATIONS

Chapter Objectives

After completing this chapter, you should be able to:

- Identify typical situations where giving and receiving feedback may be difficult.

- Use the basic steps for effectively giving and receiving feedback to handle difficult situations.

Identifying Difficult Feedback Situations

Let's face it, some feedback situations can be especially difficult. Providing redirection to someone with a "difficult" personality or accepting redirection from someone who speaks in vague generalities can leave you feeling frustrated and demoralized.

However, difficult feedback situations can end positively. You can take control of even the most unpleasant, awkward feedback situations by following the basic steps discussed in this workbook. You should review those steps when you face situations such as:

- Redirecting a staff member whose performance problems are compounded by personal problems, such as a recent divorce or financial difficulties.

- Redirecting staff members with difficult personalities.

- Redirecting a co-worker whose work habits disturb you.

- Receiving redirection from someone who uses such broad generalities that you can't figure out what the issue is.

When Personal Problems Affect Performance

It may be awkward to redirect a staff member whom you know is having personal problems. Yet accepting poor performance doesn't help the person or your organization. You and others may even be tempted to help the person do his or her job. But you and others should not take on too much of your feedback recipient's workload. Instead, discuss ways you can help resolve the problem when you create the action plan in Step Five of the giving feedback process. Because your feedback recipient is under stress, be prepared for some atypical responses, such as shouting, crying or blaming. Emphasize that you are not trying to create more stress for your recipient. You only want to help that person perform his or her job.

Step 1: Describe the behavior or performance you want to redirect.

"Brad, several outside callers have indicated that you haven't returned their voice mail messages. We really put a priority on returning calls to the public. Is something keeping you from doing this?"

Step 2: Listen to your recipient's reaction.

"I've been finding it difficult to focus because I'm getting a divorce and our child custody hear-

ing is next week. I just don't see how you can expect me to concentrate until this is all over."

Step 3: Explain the negative influence of your recipient's actions.

"Our organization prides itself on returning calls within 24 hours. When you don't return calls within that time frame, your calls end up going to someone else. Several staff members have complained about taking your calls. This not only has a negative influence on morale, but it also weakens our service to the public. I really think we have a problem here. Do you?"

Step 4: Help your recipient acknowledge that a problem exists and take responsibility for it.

"I would think you could be a little more understanding at a time like this. I promise you as soon as this whole mess is over, I'll be on top of things again."

The feedback recipient is not ready to acknowledge, or does not yet understand, that a problem exists, and he has responsibility for correcting it. At this point, the person giving the feedback needs to point out the consequences of allowing the problem to continue.

Supervisor: *"Everybody on our staff is already working at top capacity, and it's unfair to ask them to carry part of your responsibility. We need you to return all of your own calls within 24 hours starting today, or I'll have to take disciplinary action."*

Brad: *"Could this affect my pay increase that's scheduled to begin next month?"*

Supervisor: *"Yes, it could. Do you agree that we have a problem?"*

Brad: *"Well, yes, I guess we do have a problem.*

I need that additional money to cover child support."

Step 5: Develop a plan for future action.
"All right then, I'd suggest that starting today you keep up with all outside calls and return all of them within 24 hours."

Step 6: Thank your feedback recipient.
"Thank you, Brad. I realize that you're dealing with a lot right now, which makes it all the more important to maintain a good performance record at work."

When Personalities Clash

We've all met people with difficult personalities. Some seem to become angry at the slightest provocation. They get away with a lot because no one wants to say or do anything that will set them off. Others appear to have no reaction whatsoever. You may find yourself wondering if they heard a thing you said.

People like these can be a challenge to work with in the best of circumstances. If you have had unpleasant interactions with them in the past, you may be especially reluctant to give them redirection. Remember that following the basic steps can help you reach even the most difficult personality.

It can be especially challenging to redirect a noncommunicative person who finds it difficult to engage in dialogue. Your goal is to get the person to admit that a problem exists and take an active role in developing the action plan to solve it. Once you've described the problem, you may need to wait a while for the person's reaction (Step 2). Be patient. Let the other person see that you will not leave without some type of response:

You: *"So, do you understand what the situation is?"*

Recipient: *"Yes, I guess so."*

You: *"How would you describe it, then? In your own words —"*

When he responds, listen carefully (Step 2). Then explain the negative influence of your recipient's actions (Step 3). Once you are satisfied that a noncommunicative person truly understands the nature of a problem and acknowledges responsibility for it (Step 4), go to the next step. Begin to involve him or her in developing an action plan for its solution (Step 5). Again, you will have to be patient. Ask questions to be sure that the individual understands exactly what steps he or she should take to improve the behavior or performance. Finally, thank your feedback recipient (Step 6).

On the opposite end of the communication scale, people who usually over-react may cry, yell, or become defensive in response to your redirection. Don't let them use this behavior to take control of the situation. Remain calm and continue to focus on the steps until they acknowledge their role in the problem—even if a recipient's response attacks you personally:

Recipient: *"You've had it in for me ever since I joined this organization. This is just another of your attempts to get rid of me."*

You: *"We're talking about specific behaviors you demonstrate when working with other staff, not about whether anyone is out to get you. When you complain frequently, miss key deadlines, don't answer your E-mail, and interrupt others during meetings or conversations, you make it difficult for others to get their work done. Do you understand why others perceive you as being uncooperative?"*

When a Co-worker's Personal Habits Affect Your Work

It may seem trivial, but sometimes people's work habits and personal grooming can affect others in their work environment. Some of the most common problems of this type involve:

- Loud gum chewing

- Dirty coffee mugs left in others' offices or common areas

- Bad breath, body odor, or strong perfume/cologne

- Incessant personal phone calls

- Sloppy or inappropriate dress

One of the most difficult things you will ever have to do is to tell another person that his body odor or perfume/cologne is overpowering. However, you may need to provide this very personal kind of feedback if the problem is affecting your ability to do your job. Remember that you are doing the other person, yourself, and everyone else in the work area a favor—although it will be difficult to keep that in perspective at the time.

Don't feel the need to develop this type of redirection to the same extent that you do others. You do not need to get your feedback recipient to accept responsibility for the problem or develop an action plan. Simply state your feedback in the most polite way you can and allow the other person to deal with it privately:

You: *"I really like your perfume, but because we have to work together so closely, there are days when it gets a little strong for me. I've been wondering if you could wear a little less of it."*

Because these problems are so personal, you should present this type of redirection in a private setting where your conversation cannot be overheard. Some feedback recipients may become defensive or display hurt feelings, while others will want to talk about the problem. Every situation is different—just try to approach each one sensitively. You might ask yourself if the feedback recipient would feel more comfortable if he or she received this information from someone of the same sex. You also should present this type of feedback as your response or coming from you. Don't say something like "everybody's been complaining." This will only make your feedback recipient feel that he or she has been the focus of work jokes.

When You Receive Overly General Redirection

It's difficult to remember that all feedback can be valuable when you receive redirection that is vague and unfocused. But remember, no matter how badly a feedback situation starts out, you can derive some benefit from it by asking the right questions. For example, see how the following jail booking officers handle vague feedback from their supervisor.

Supervisor: *"Your performance last weekend was terrible. I'm just glad we didn't have an outright riot here. I don't know how I'm going to explain this to headquarters."*

Officer 1: *" Excuse me. I can see you're upset, but could you please explain what exactly you're upset about?"*

Supervisor: *"What do you mean, what am I upset about? Saturday was terrible."*

Officer 2: *"But what was terrible about it? We were booking them as fast as possible."*

Officer 3: *"Did we process some of them incorrectly?*

Supervisor: *"No, that was okay. It was the long line, and all of the confusion."*

Officer 3: *"We thought that ran pretty smoothly."*

Supervisor: *"Smoothly! You had people everywhere—there didn't seem to be any movement around lunchtime at all!"*

Officer 3: *"I'm sorry. We got our lunch breaks confused and were shorthanded for a little while."*

Supervisor: *"Well, why don't you post a sign-up sheet so that you can see who goes when?"*

Officer 2: *"That's a very good idea. We'll do that today."*

Take Control of the Situation

These are just a few of the difficult feedback situations you might encounter on the job—you have probably encountered many others! But remember, no matter how awkward or unpleasant a feedback situation may appear at first, you can take control and turn it into something positive.

Chapter Seven Review

Suggested answers appear on page 98.

1. List four difficult feedback situations in which you can use the basic steps.

    _____

    _____

    _____

    _____

2. **True/False.** If a co-worker or staff member has a personal problem, you should do as much of his or her work as possible.

3. **True/False.** Your goal in redirecting a noncommunicative person is to help him or her learn how to have a conversation.

4. **True/False.** When you're redirecting a co-worker about a personal habit, you don't need to get him or her to accept responsibility for the problem or develop an action plan.

5. **True/False.** By asking the right questions, you can benefit from vague or unfocused feedback.

Chapter Eight

DEVELOPING YOUR FEEDBACK SKILLS

Chapter Objectives

After completing this chapter, you should be able to:

- Reassess your current feedback skills.
- Create an action plan for improving your feedback skills.

Reassessing Your Feedback Skills

At the beginning of this workbook, you had the opportunity to assess your current feedback skills. Now it's time to develop an action plan for improving your weak areas.

The following statements represent feedback skills that you have learned about in this workbook. Mark each statement that you would like to include in your personal action plan.

Action Plan for Giving Feedback Effectively

☐   I will pick an appropriate time and place to give feedback.

☐   I will keep my emotions in check, remain calm and professional, and keep my voice even.

☐   I will provide specific, detailed information about the staff member's behavior or performance.

☐   I will explain the influence the staff member's actions are having on the team or organization.

☐   I will really listen to the responses of those receiving my feedback.

☐   I will clarify my expectations if there is any confusion about the action in question.

☐   I will remember to thank and encourage the receivers of my feedback.

☐   I will provide input as needed in developing an action plan for meeting behavioral or performance goals.

☐   I will focus on the steps of the feedback process to keep the conversation on track.

☐   I will try to understand feedback from the other person's point of view and preferred communication style.

Action Plan for Receiving Feedback Effectively

☐   I will truly listen to what feedback givers are saying.

☐   I will keep feedback in perspective and won't overreact.

☐   I will listen in all feedback situations.

☐   I will try to learn from feedback—even if it's given poorly.

☐   I will admit to and learn from questions about my performance or behavior at work.

☐   I will attempt to turn every feedback session into a useful encounter.

☐   I will accept redirection and reinforcement rather than denying them.

☐   I will accept responsibility for my role in achieving individual, team, and organizational goals.

☐   I will accept responsibility for developing solutions to performance and behavioral problems that threaten my personal and work goals.

☐   I will accept responsibility for keeping my emotions in check during feedback discussions.

Developing an Action Plan

Take some time now to develop an action plan for improving the skills that you checked. There are any number of ways that you can develop your skills for giving and receiving feedback. Here are a few you might try:

- Identify another person in your organization who you believe gives and receives feedback effectively and observe that person. Take note of the things that person does which makes his or her feedback effective. Then try to develop those actions yourself.

- Is there a person in your organization at your level (not a staff member or an offender you supervise) to whom you frequently give feedback? Ask that person to rate your skills. Do you give that person enough information so that he can effectively improve his behavior and performance? Or, is he often confused by your feedback? Based on the person's response, determine which feedback skills you need to improve.

- Is there a person in your organization who frequently gives you feedback? Do you accept that person's feedback with an open mind, or do you become defensive and make excuses? Ask that person to rate your skills as a feedback recipient, and determine the things you can do to improve those skills.

- Talk to someone in your organization who deals with feedback situations effectively, and ask that person to be your mentor. You might try role-playing feedback situations with that person so that you can practice both giving and receiving feedback in a comfortable environment.

- Learn more about feedback and communication skills. There are a number of resources you can tap into both locally and nationally, including the American Correctional Association.

- Practice your feedback skills whenever possible. Don't shy away from the need to respond to another staff member's behavior or performance, and encourage your co-workers to do the same for you.

As you consider these options, choose two or three that you would like to create an action plan for in the next few weeks. Your plan could look something like this:

- Ask Ryan whether I have been giving him useful feedback about his supervision of staff. Ask him if there are suggestions I haven't been giving him that he would find useful.

- Observe how my supervisor gives me feedback during our next review. Make note of the techniques that I like and don't like and compare them to the way I give feedback to my co-workers and the staff I supervise.

- Ask Charlene to help me role play a re-direction session. Ask her to pretend to be defensive so that I can practice dealing with excuses.

After you've had a few months to develop your skills, take the self-assessment at the beginning of this workbook again, and see whether you score differently. With a little practice, you'll soon be able to give your staff, co-workers, and supervisors useful feedback. And, you'll be able to effectively receive feedback that will help you achieve your personal and professional goals.

Chapter Review Answers

Chapter One

1. Workplace feedback is information we provide co-workers and supervisors about their job performance and work related behavior.

2. Three types of ineffective workplace feedback are:
   1. Silence
   2. Criticism
   3. Praise

3. Two types of effective workplace feedback are redirection and reinforcement.

4. Effective workplace feedback has a number of traits. Three of these are:
   1. acts directed towards the future
   2. goal oriented
   3. multidirectional, supportive and ongoing

Chapter Two

1. Detailed feedback is specific, accurate, and inquiring.

2. In order to provide your feedback recipient with as much specific detail as possible, you should provide reinforcement and redirection as close as possible to the time the act in question occurred.

3. Specifying is the process of giving specific and detailed information to your recipient.

4. Probing is the process of requesting detailed information about behaviors or performance.

Chapter Three

1. True. Because it takes time to think through all the issues related to giving feedback, you may find yourself putting more time into planning your feedback than you do actually giving it.

2. False. It is necessary to identify and describe specific actions that you want to redirect or reinforce. Your feedback recipient needs detailed feedback in order to know which actions to repeat and which to change.

3. True.

4. True.

5. False. Delayed feedback is more difficult to give than timely feedback. It is always easier to give redirection or reinforcement when the action in question is fresh in everyone's mind.

Chapter Four

1. False. Redirection and reinforcement should be scheduled to make sure neither you or your feedback recipient will be too tired or stressed and there will be no interruptions.

2. False. You should never redirect and individual in front of other staff. Doing so might create hostility and embarrassment.

3. Four basic steps for providing reinforcement include:
    1. Describe the behavior or performance you want to reinforce
    2. Explain the positive impact that act has had on the organization.
    3. Help the receiver of your feedback take credit for his or her success.
    4. Thank the receiver of your feedback for his or her contribution.

4. Six basic steps for providing redirection include:
    1. Describe the behavior or performance you want to redirect.
    2. Listen to the other person's response.
    3. Clarify your expectations or provide examples to illustrate your points.
    4. Help your feedback recipient acknowledge that a problem exists and take responsibility for his or her actions.
    5. Develop a plan for future action.
    6. Thank your feedback recipient.

5. True.

Chapter Five

1. True.

2. True.

3. True.

4. False. Eye contact is important in any face-to-face encounter. Try to maintain eye contact with the person giving you feedback, even if you feel awkward.

5. The four basic steps for effectively receiving feedback include:
   1. Ask for details.
   2. Paraphrase what you think you
      heard.
   3. Seek suggestions for future action.
   4. Thank the person for his or her feed
      back.

6. True.

7. True.

Chapter Six

1. Match each communication style with
   the appropriate description.
   A. Detail-oriented, accurate
      (2. Investigator)
   B. Direct, task oriented
      (4. Driver)
   C. Supportive, avoids change and
      confrontation
      (3. Contributor)
   D. Relationship-oriented, enthusiastic
      (1. Collaborator)

2. In order to fully appreciate others'
   communication styles, you must first
   understand and appreciate your own.

3. You should match the individual's style.
   Deliver or receive feedback in a way
   that is comfortable to the other person.

Chapter Seven

1. Four difficult feedback situations where you can use the basic steps are:
   A. Redirecting a staff member whose performance problems are compounded by personal problems, such as a recent divorce or financial difficulties.
   B. Redirecting staff members whose work habits disturb you.
   C. Redirecting staff members with difficult personalities.
   D. Receiving redirection from someone who uses such broad generalizations that you can't figure out what the issue is.

2. False. You should discuss ways to help resolve the problem.

3. False. Your goal should be to get the person to admit that a problem exists and take an active role in developing the action plan to solve it.

4. False. Although difficult, you still need to get the person to accept responsibility and develop an action plan.

5. True.